We Are All Different

We All Communicate

Rebecca Rissman

www.heinemannlibrary.co.uk
Visit our website to find out more information about Heinemann Library books.

To order:
☎ Phone 44 (0) 1865 888066
📄 Send a fax to 44 (0) 1865 314091
💻 Visit the Heinemann Bookshop at www.heinemannlibrary.co.uk to browse our catalogue and order online.

Heinemann Library is an imprint of Capstone Global Library Limited, a company incorporated in England and Wales having its registered office at 7 Pilgrim Street, London, EC4V 6LB – Registered company number: 6695582

Heinemann is a registered trademark of Pearson Education Limited, under licence to Capstone Global Library Limited

Edited by Rebecca Rissman, Charlotte Guillain and Catherine Veitch
Designed by Joanna Hinton-Malivoire
Picture research by Tracy Cummins
Production by Duncan Gilbert
Originated by Dot Gradations Ltd
Printed and bound in China by South China Printing Company Ltd

ISBN 978 0 431 19310 6 (hardback)
13 12 11 10 09
10 9 8 7 6 5 4 3 2 1

ISBN 978 0 431 19316 8 (paperback)
14 13 12 11 10
10 9 8 7 6 5 4 3 2 1

British Library Cataloguing in Publication Data
Rissman, Rebecca
We all communicate. - (We are all different)
1. People with disabilities - Means of communication - Juvenile literature
305.9'08
A full catalogue record for this book is available from the British Library.

Acknowledgements
We would like to thank the following for permission to reproduce photographs: ©agefotostock pp. **16** (Image Source/Royalty Free), **20** (John Birdsall); ©drr.net pp. **10** (Borut Peterlin), **11** (Huntstock.com), **14** (enzodalverme.com), **15** (Image Source Ltd.), **23 bottom** (enzodalverme.com); ©Getty Images pp. **4** (Ryan McVay), **7** (Chris Cheadle), **9** (David Deas), **13** (Paul Viant), **19** (Jacobs Stock Photography); ©Heinemann Raintree p. **6** (Richard Hutchings); ©istockphoto p. **17** (ranplett); ©Jupiter Images p. **21** (Comma Image); ©PhotoEdit pp. **22** (Michael Newman), **23 middle** (Michael Newman); ©Shutterstock pp. **8** (Amra Pasic), **12** (Ronen), **23 top** (Ronen).

Cover photograph of hearing and speech impaired students interacting with each other using sign language reproduced with permission of ©AP Photo (Mahesh Kumar A). Back cover photograph of a family talking reproduced with permission of ©Shutterstock (Rob Marmion).

Every effort has been made to contact copyright holders of material reproduced in this book. Any omissions will be rectified in subsequent printings if notice is given to the publishers.

Contents

Differences

We are all different ages and sizes. We all have different coloured hair and skin. We are all good at different things.

Communicating

People communicate in different ways.

People understand in different ways.

Listening

Sometimes people listen to
loud sounds.

Sometimes people listen to
quiet sounds.

Sometimes people listen to their teacher.

Sometimes people listen to their friends.

headphones

Sometimes people listen to
a television.

Sometimes people listen to a radio.

Talking

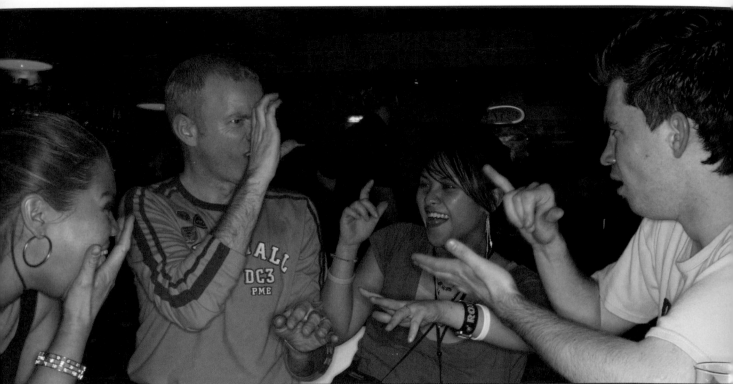

People talk in different ways. Some people talk using sign language.

People talk in different places.

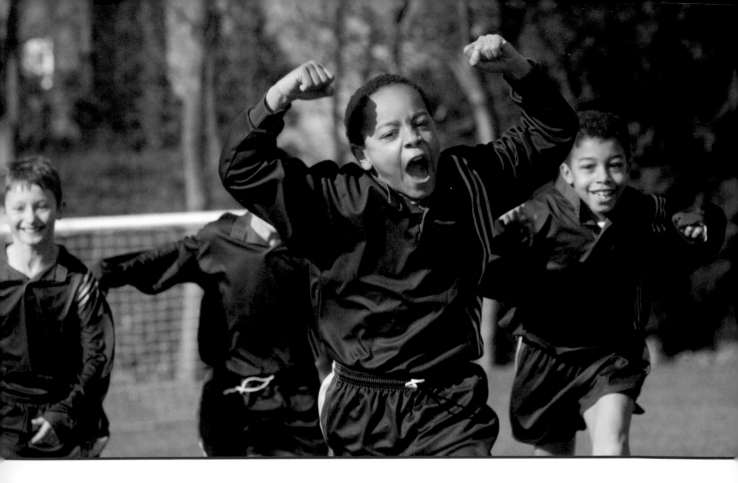

Sometimes people shout in
loud voices.

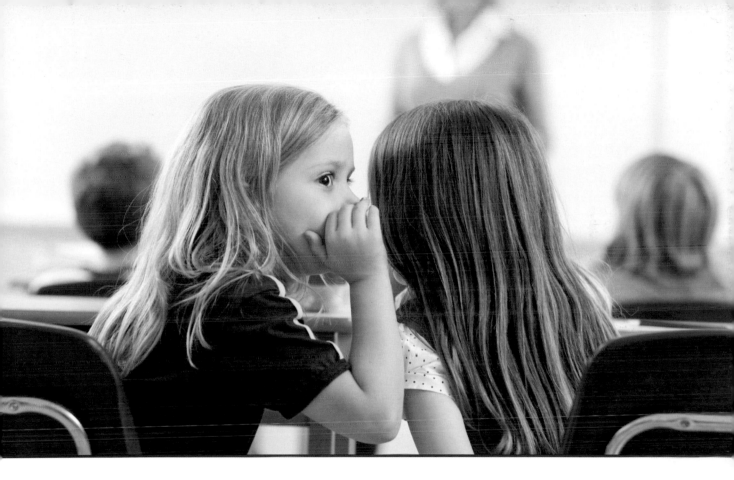

Sometimes people whisper in soft voices.

Sometimes people talk to their family.

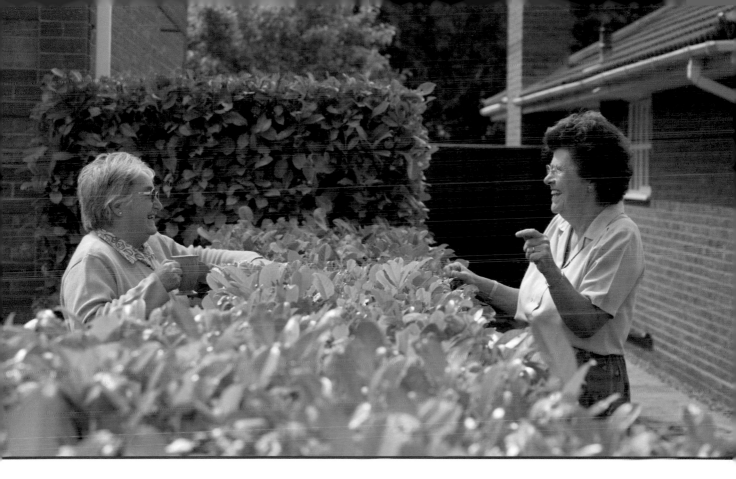

Sometimes people talk to their neighbours.

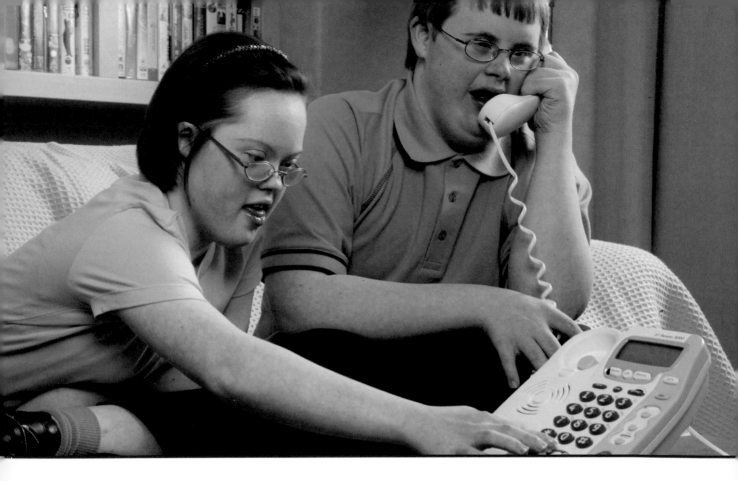

Sometimes people talk on
the telephone.

Sometimes people talk on
the computer.

We are all different

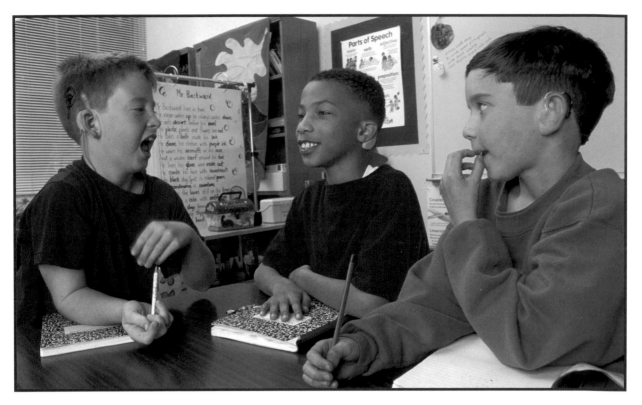

We are all different.

How do you talk? How do you listen?

Words to know

 headphones small speakers people wear over or inside the ears. Headphones help people hear.

 hearing aid small machine that helps people hear. Hearing aids fit inside and behind the ear.

 sign language way to talk with hand signs

This section includes related vocabulary words that can help children learn about this topic. Use these words to explore communication.

Index

Note to parents and teachers

Before reading
Talk with children about the ways we are the same and different. Discuss how some of the differences are physical or mental and some are because different people like different things, but that all people are special and all people are equally important.

After reading
Ask children to list as many ways to communicate as they can think of (e.g. writing emails, talking on the telephone, sign language). Then ask the children to vote on their favourite way to communicate. Record the answers on the board.